Stephanie Be

Nine Strategies for Dealing with the Difficult Stuff

Finding calm in the eye of the storm

Contents

Dedication

This book is a labour of love. It was inspired by a good friend who was going through some tough times and asked me for suggestions on handling them – thank you for asking. It is written with immense gratitude to everyone who helped me through some of the most difficult times of my life; you are too many to name but you know who you are. I also have such gratitude to my family for the ways we have loved and supported one another through the challenges we have experienced. I dedicate this book to my mother, Joanne Innes. Thank you for loving me so well and for living with such courage for so long. You continue to inspire me.

Invitation

Thank-you so much for buying my book. I've poured my heart into it and I hope that it brings you comfort and provides you with practical strategies. If you are interested in hearing more of my experiences and perspective, please sign up for my newsletter at Stephanieberryman.com. On my blog, I share my reflections about life, parenting, relationships, work and how we choose to engage with the world. When you sign up for my newsletter, you also receive my free e-book 'The Seven Essential Elements of a Good Life'.

Dealing with the Difficult Stuff

If you are reading this book, you are likely going through some difficult times. I'm sorry that you're having a tough time. I hope that this book helps you, not just with some strategies and ideas, but also as a reminder that you are not alone. We are all in the same boat. We will all have struggles in our lives, some of us for a brief and temporary time, others over a lifetime. If nothing else, the challenging times remind us to revel in the good times.

If you're going through a challenging time, it will not last forever. This too shall pass. When things were at their darkest, I actually wrote this phrase out on a post-it note and put it on my front door. It helped me remember that both the good times and the tough times would pass so I should appreciate and enjoy what was good and sweet in those moments.

I hope this book provides comfort, strategies, and a different perspective on the struggles we experience. In every challenge is an offering - if we are open to it. We grow and learn and become who we are by facing the tough stuff in our lives and walking through it the best way we know how.

My experience with the difficult stuff:

Whenever I open up and share a difficult situation I'm going through with another person, they often have a story to tell in return, either from the past or the present. This book is my way of sharing my stories. I offer them out to you because we all need to connect, to know and feel that we are not alone, and that we will come out the other side of our challenges intact. Most of the experiences I write about happened years ago; in the now, I feel blessed to be in a really wonderful time of life. I'm married to the love of my life, and we have two young, healthy, happy kids. I'm doing work that I love.

That said, I still have challenges – I haven't slept through the night in five years (thanks to those two happy healthy kids who I am so grateful for), I often feel overwhelmed, I've had some health challenges recently, two good friends have passed away in the past few years. Because of my experience years ago with some incredibly difficult times, I learned a number of strategies to help me cope with what I'm experiencing now. I am grateful to have the perspective that what I'm experiencing now feels mild and manageable in contrast to the intensity of what my life was like a decade ago. Coming through hard times can give us a different perspective on what we face after them and that is a gift.

Challenges and richness can co-exist in a life and, if we're managing the difficult stuff well, they will. I know there will be more challenges ahead because that's life, but I am appreciating this time so much more because of all that came before it.

My experience of the difficult stuff started when I was quite young. At five years old, my brother Joel was born. Instead of the happy and joyful event that was anticipated, it was the beginning of a complex journey woven through with shots of wild happiness, deep beauty, and a love between us so sweet and sure. Joel was born with severe cerebral palsy. Unbeknownst to me, the doctors had told my parents he wouldn't live past the age of three. His first years of life were filled with harrowing seizures, panicked trips to the hospital, and the constant sense that he was living on the edge of death. Even at my young age, I could feel both his fragility and his strength. He lived well past those predicted three years. He lived a good, rich life filled with friends and family who loved him deeply and who he loved immensely. He never walked, never spoke, and continued to have seizures and spasms much of his life, and he was one of the happiest people I have ever known.

I am so grateful Joel was my brother - as much as it broke my heart to see him hurting - without him, I would have missed out on a whole world of love, happiness, strength, sorrow and learning. My brother and his boundless capacity for love, his hunger for all that life offered, and his indomitable spirit taught me so much and gave me far more than I ever could have had without him.

People often comment that I am a positive, optimistic, and glass half-full kind of person. I grew up with a vivid reminder of how fortunate I was to do even the most basic things - run, eat my favourite foods, dress myself, speak. I also grew up with a deep sorrow that my brother would never have those gifts. As we aged,

I also saw the sweetness in his life - the deep love and relationships he had with close friends, caregivers and family, the incredible joy he took from life, his great sense of humour and his laughter. He taught me much about the complicated relationship we have with the difficult stuff. It brings us gifts as well as challenges.

When I was 11 years old, my mother was diagnosed with stage IV throat cancer. She was 37, with four young children. As I lay in bed - tearful and terrified - the night before her diagnosis, my mom came in and promised me that she wouldn't have cancer. She broke that promise and with that, my heart. Next she promised me she wouldn't die. A brave promise for a stage IV cancer patient who had been given a 10% chance of survival. She delivered, and with that, she healed my broken heart. She also taught me the power of will: she absolutely refused to die. She suffered through harrowing radiation and surgery, experienced terrible side effects, and never gave up.

Years later, she told me of a vision she had while in the hospital: a man dressed completely in white stood at the end of her bed for four days. He wore a white suit, white dress shoes, and a white gabardine hat. He said nothing; he just stood there, waiting. She sensed his kindness and knew he had come to take her to the other side. She told me that she kept saying "not yet", and he finally went away.

Ten years later she and my alcoholic father divorced. I, as the oldest and only daughter, became her primary caregiver. While she maintained relatively good health for quite a few years after the cancer, the extreme treatment eventually caught up with her. Her thyroid stopped producing. She had to quit her beloved job managing a university bookstore. Her jaw had to be replaced; she endured painful and complicated surgery to graft a part of her hip to her jaw. She was in recovery for months and spent many more walking with a cane.

Around the time I became responsible for her care, my mother needed a tube inserted into her stomach to help her avoid a choking response due to a damaged esophagus. I returned home to our prairie city from the coast, at the ripe old age of 21, to talk to doctors and learn the language of tubes, feeds and clearing blockages. After her operation I remember pushing her down the hallway in her wheelchair and her saying to me with an apology in her voice, "I think we are both a little young for this." She was 47.

12 years later she was dead. But she didn't give up in those intervening years. She knew, more than any of us, that life was short, and for her, likely shorter than most. This made her more determined than ever to live and to live well. How could this not influence me? Her fierce determination to survive and to have a good life was the filter through which I weighed many of my decisions. What was really important in life? Was this next step worthy of my one wild and precious life? I have always lived with the knowledge of death and the inspiration of family members who fought so hard to delay it.

This knowledge put my priorities in the right place. I knew from a very young age that the people we love are the most important thing in the world. I also learned early on that life could turn on a dime, as it had for my mother. She was vibrant and healthy one moment, working and parenting and visiting friends, and the next moment, she was fighting for her life, tubes and machines surrounding her, lying tiny in her hospital bed.

After some time caring for my mother, she encouraged me to return to my life on the coast, far from our prairie town, to travel and have the adventures I had always wanted. She wanted a big life for me and I leapt at it. Had I not watched her and Joel struggle for what most of us take for granted, I may have stayed home feeling duty bound to care for her. Instead, I felt duty bound to go live that big life and explore the opportunities I was fortunate enough to be able to experience.

My mother stayed in our small prairie town for another year after her surgery, adjusting to life with a feeding tube. Then it occurred to her that this tube did not define her and did not tie her to one place. She made an incredibly brave decision. She decided to move to a small town in Mexico, one filled with expats. She went to the town of Ajijic with her feeding tube, ten boxes of formula, her complex medical conditions, and her pills. Most able-bodied single women in their fifties would shy away from living abroad but she knew what she wanted – warmth, time, and the space to relax and enjoy her forced retirement.

My mom finally did break her promise when she passed away at 59. Not from the cancer but from Alzheimer's. In the 22 years in between that first promise and her death she lived the life she wanted.

Alzheimer's disease is a slow forgetting. A slow forgetting not just of who your children are and what you love most in the world, but also of how the coffee maker works and whether bath beads are for the bath or if they're maybe candies. It is agonizing. My mother could no longer handle her own medical care, so I managed her feeding tube, her medications and all her appointments. Her final three years were a devastating and heartbreaking falling away of the woman I knew and loved. During that time, my brother Joel passed away. Losing him opened a flood of grief I wasn't prepared for.

Add into the mix an alcoholic father and a brother who was diagnosed with bipolar disorder and addictions at the age of 19. My brother has fought his battle with mental illness as fiercely as my mother fought hers with cancer. He continues to surface but the road he has travelled has been a heart-wrenching one for all of us. I have loved him and supported him as best I could through the years of his illness; I have felt the devastation of him spiraling away from his centre, the cautiously hope of watching him return to himself, and the disappointment of seeing him slip away again. I have learned more than I can say from his strength, his courage and his resilience.

My family has taught me an immense amount about dealing with the difficult stuff. When you include the regular stuff of life such as relationship break-ups, beloved grandparents and friends passing away, moving cities, and figuring out work, love and making my way in the world, I feel like I could get a PhD in figuring out how to get through the difficult stuff.

On that note, I have no professional designations whatsoever that qualify me to be sharing advice. I'm an English major not a counsellor. I just love to write and share what I have experienced with the hopes that it may help others.

Everything passes and changes. My father has been in recovery for 21 years, and my brother is managing his mental health and maintaining a stable life. I'm so grateful for these gifts, far more grateful because of the hard times we have been through.

I know that your version of the difficult stuff will be different than mine. One of the most valuable things I learned at a grief workshop was to let go of comparisons. Whatever we are going through, it is painful. The feelings are the same - hurt, anger, sorrow, and grief. It's what we do with those feelings, and how we come through the tough times, that will shape us. Here are some of the strategies I've used over the years to deal with the difficult stuff, I hope you will find them helpful.

Nine Strategies for Dealing with the Difficult Stuff

1. Feel your feelings

Feelings your feelings is one of the most challenging things to do when going through tough stuff. I cried a lot in the first few weeks after my brother died. And then, after that, I didn't want to feel any more so I buried myself in watching season after season of *24*. I wanted to avoid the tears. My grief counsellor recommended I start watching *6 Feet Under*. Each episode starts with a death: in those first five minutes I sobbed my heart out. It gave me an opening to feel, for a few moments, the incredible grief I was experiencing. Then, *6 Feet Under* took me out of it, allowing me to follow the story. It was exactly what I needed at the time.

You need to create space and conditions for your feelings, especially if you are too busy dealing with the difficult stuff to feel anything at all. Look at photos, listen to music, go to a support group or a counsellor, or talk to a friend. If nothing else, call your local crisis line and talk about what is happening in your life. A listening and compassionate ear is often all we need to let our feelings come up. When we feel them, rather than repressing them, we can move on.

I didn't want to cry after Joel died because I felt that once I started I would never stop. Whenever I did give my tears the space I cried myself out within an hour or two, and then I always felt much better. I know we can't feel our feelings all the time, but don't numb out permanently. Lots of us use TV, sex, booze, work, or other drugs to avoid our feelings. Yes, you need occasional escapes from the challenges in life and all the associated emotions. But - if you avoid your feelings forever - they will catch up with you, and either provoke more difficult stuff or spill out in inappropriate times and ways.

Conversely, if your feelings are ever-present, then sometimes you need to give yourself a break from their intensity. This is different than avoiding them. Three weeks after my mother died, I went to a meditation retreat; I asked the teacher about managing my grief. When she learned how fresh it was, she suggested very gently that I both experience it and allow myself a reprieve. "Go see a movie," she suggested kindly. You know yourself better than anyone else, so listen to your instincts and follow them: your instincts will let you know when you need to feel the depth of your feelings, and when you need to give yourself a rest.

Whatever you do, make the time and space to feel your feelings, so you can let them go. It takes courage to feel the depth of the pain, but when you do, you come through it more whole and stronger.

2. Get support

When you are going through tough stuff, lean on your friends and support networks. Here's a radical idea - ask for help. It's sad that this is such a radical idea, but I so often see people struggling to ask for help. We are raised in a culture that expects self-sufficiency. Not only is this unrealistic, but those who care about us want to help and feel useful. Give them the opportunity, even if it's just taking you for coffee, to an appointment or helping you get groceries. When someone says "What can I do to help?" don't turn the offer away: find some way for them to help.

When my mother was diagnosed with Alzheimer's, I was single and lived, along with my mom, in a different city from the rest of the family. I leaned on friends and anyone who offered help, because I knew I needed it. I was working full time in a demanding job and totally over my head in caring for my mom's many medical needs.

The mother of one of my friends offered to come and sit with my mother once a week. I leapt on it. An old friend of my parents' offered the same, and I gratefully accepted. We are not islands. We need each other. Now that we often live far from our families, we need to rely on friends as if they were family. Challenging times will help you identify who is there for you and who is not. My thinking is that if people can't show up during the difficult times, you need to let them go. It doesn't mean you can't reconnect at a later point, but during tough times, you need people who can support you.

Don't judge the people who can't be there for you; they may have their own stuff going on, or they may just not be emotionally prepared to enter the world you are in. I had a few friends step away when my mom had Alzheimer's and my brother was dying. I totally get it. I would have run from that situation if I could have!

If you don't have good friends in your life or if they can't be there for you right now, don't give up and feel like you have to do everything on your own. There are options. With my mother, I connected with the Alzheimer's Society; they provided a weekly afternoon program for her and a support group for me. After my brother died, I went to see a grief counsellor. After my mom died, I went to both a grief retreat and counsellor.

I did everything I could to connect with people that would help me get through. I've found that for many situations, I can talk to a close friend and get the support I need, but when dealing with my grief or with medical conditions, I needed more than a listening friend. I needed someone who understood the situation or was an expert in the field.

Figure out what support you need and find a way to get it. Call your local crisis line. They are free, trained, and able to offer you caring support. They may also be able to help you identify and connect with resources, including excellent free ones.

3. Find somewhere else for the love to go

If you are losing someone to a disease or have lost someone to death or a break up - and your heart is broken - the gift is that you loved someone deeply. I remember many years ago a friend of mine lost his father suddenly. He seemed completely unfazed by it and went about the business of funerals and estate settlement with no emotion. When my brother died, I cried for months and could barely cope with life, so I didn't understand my friend's reaction. I felt certain that he was simply avoiding his grief. So I asked him about his feelings; he explained to me that his father had left the family years earlier, and he really didn't love him. He had no grief because there was no love. He envied my sorrow, because it came from a close and loving relationship with my brother. This completely changed my perspective on my grief; it was a gift rather than a burden.

At the grief workshop I attended, I learned that when we lose a person we feel lost, because all this love we have for them has nowhere to go. We can go crazy with grief and never find our way out of it, or we can find a way to redirect the love we have for that person.

We also may have a sense of loss and grief after a breakup. I remember a time in my mid-twenties when I was obsessing about a boyfriend after a break-up, and I couldn't stop thinking about him. I realized that I was giving him all my energy and power and love, when really I should be giving it to myself because I was going through such a tough time. I made a rule that every time I started to have a conversation in my head with him I had to switch to focus on myself. Instead of having useless conversations in my mind, I started thinking about what I learned from the situation as well as what I wanted to do to take care of myself.

After a death, you may want to redirect your love to something that connects you with that person. After my brother died, I started working with an organization that supported families of people with disabilities. This was so good for me because one of the ways I expressed my love for Joel was through helping people understand who Joel was and to see him as the amazing brother I loved, not just a guy in a wheelchair. I had the opportunity in my job to stay connected to people with disabilities, and also to help others see them for the amazing people that they were. Redirecting my love for Joel into work that helped me feel connected to him was a really valuable part of my healing.

4. Connect with Spirit

There are many different ways we can connect with spirit. Some people feel a deep connection to spirit and spirituality through their religion. I don't belong to an organized religion so I did what felt natural to me and what had helped me feel connected in the past.

What feeds your spirit and helps you feel whole? For me, it was writing. I wrote my way through a lot of grief, pouring it onto the pages and slowly but surely finding my way. I also went out into nature as often as I could, where I felt closest to my spirit, to my mother's and my brother's spirit, to God. I heard an interview the other day with a professional musician who had lost his father at the age of twelve. To manage his grief, he played the cello and it helped him feel closer to his own spirit and to express feelings he couldn't articulate. Figure out what helps you connect with yourself and make time to do it. We all have something that helps us connect with spirit, for the cellist it was music, for me it was writing. If you don't know, this could be an excellent opportunity to find out. Try things and see what helps you connect with yourself and your feelings. You'll know it when you've found it.

Rely on your spiritual beliefs, whatever they are. I believe the spirits of my loved ones are still with me. This has given me great comfort and the ability to still feel the love and connection I had with them when they were alive. A very wise, religious friend of mine suggested that faith was simply having something to believe in. He said, "It doesn't matter if it's true or not, what matters is simply that we believe." It was so freeing. I had always felt that the spirits of those who pass on live on in our hearts. I clung to that in the heartbreaking dark nights when I ached with the physical loss.

I think about my children and the challenges they experience. I know that all I can do is support them through it. I can't fix it or change it, but I can be there and love them. This is what spiritual belief can do for us; it can give us love and comfort as we go through our challenges. I watch my kids as they struggle with situations beyond their control, whether it's something as minor as a lost toy or something more wrenching, like the loss of a friendship. And I want so much to fix it for them, but I know there is nothing I can do. I also know that, even if I could fix it, I wouldn't be helping them to learn, grow, and experience life and their feelings fully. So, I hold them when they cry, and tell them I understand how hard it is and that I know they'll be ok. I imagine this is how God looks upon us - with so much love and compassion - knowing that we have to experience this, and that we will get through.

My journey with my brother and his mental illness taught me to surrender. I had to stop trying to rescue him and just stand helpless in the face of what he experiences. It is humbling and occasionally terrifying and heartbreaking, but I have to trust that it is his journey. So I pray, usually to my mother and brother, to be with him in the dark nights of the soul, to help him know that he has courage and strength, and that he is deeply loved. All I can do is send healing thoughts to him and trust that he will find his way.

Another thought that has helped me is that I don't know what the big picture is. I do not mean to say that "everything happens for a reason." Not only do I disagree with this, but I also feel it's one of the most thoughtless and insensitive things to say to someone who is struggling with difficult stuff, particularly a serious loss. Maybe there's a reason, maybe there isn't. Sometimes, terrible things just happen, and it is absolutely heartbreaking. The big picture is that maybe this heartbreak will break our hearts open, and it will support us to make different choices. Maybe we have lost a job or a relationship, and, in that moment, it feels like things will never get better. But three years from now, looking back, we will say it's the best thing that ever happened to us. The event is not what defines us: how we respond to it does. Our spiritual connection and belief in something bigger can help us respond with trust and grace.

If you aren't connected to an organized religion, follow what feels right to you. When my brother passed, I felt his spirit with me. When my mother passed, I felt her spirit with me. It continues to feel right to believe they are with me. This faith has helped me through some of the toughest times. Those times when I've felt deeply sad that I didn't have them with me, like at my wedding, I have felt their spirit. Whatever you believe, what matters most is our faith. What matters most is that we have something to believe in. Let it carry you.

5. Let go of wanting things to be different

Although I am not a practitioner of any religion, I do take bits and pieces from various religions and incorporate them into my life. Through my meditation retreats, I have learned a few key principles of Buddhism. One that really resonates with me is the belief that we create our own suffering by wanting things to be a certain way. We need to let go and accept what is happening. In this way, we reduce our suffering, and focus our thoughts and feelings on what is happening rather than on what we wish was or wasn't happening.

I remember reading about a woman who had cancer, and her family kept saying, "It's not fair." She asked them, "What would be fair? That someone else would have it instead of me? This is just how it is. I'm not sure fair ever really enters into it." That resonated with me because it can be tempting to heap anger and disappointment at what has happened onto an already heart wrenching time. It has happened. It is unchangeable. Wishing it were different is not only a waste of energy but also can create more stress. We can get caught up in the unfairness, and keep ourselves stuck, adding to our own suffering by wishing things were different. It can drain us and prevent us from dealing with the situation.

Instead, we need to turn our minds to that which we can influence. Sometimes this means making appointments, talking to people, helping out or asking for help, or taking action to make things better. Other times you may feel helpless and that you can't do anything. Those are the times you really do have to surrender to what is happening. It can be the hardest thing to do, to just sit and say "Yes, this is happening right now. Nothing I can do will change it. I just have to go through this experience." Even though it is hard to surrender, I promise it is easier than railing out against it.

Doing this requires a lot of redirection of our thoughts. It's very easy to get caught up in the 'I can't believe this is happening, this is so unfair' spiral. When I feel I can't do anything else one of the things that I find useful is to do a loving kindness meditation either for myself or for someone I love who is going through a difficult time. Recently a good friend of mine had cancer. She lived in another city. I couldn't do much, but I did do a meditation for her every night and sent her healing energy. I also do this meditation for my brother when his mental health isn't good. For me, doing this meditation helps me do something when I feel I can't do anything else. The meditation is from the Loving Kindness (Mettha) school of Buddhism:

> May you be peaceful and happy in heart
>
> May you be safe and protected in all ways
>
> May you be strong and healthy in body (and mind) –
>
> *my addition*
>
> May you live in this world with joy and ease and gratitude

There are various versions of this meditation. This is one that I learned when my mother was in the final stages of her Alzheimer's. I found it so helpful. It helped us both journey the rocky path towards the end.

6. Build up your inner strength

When we are going through challenges, it can be tempting to be really hard on ourselves. Don't be too tough on yourself, especially if you played a role in generating your own situation. The more you berate and judge yourself, the more stuck you become. Instead, ask yourself if there is anything you can learn from the situation - and then, move on. Where we focus our attention and energy is what grows. If we focus on being compassionate to ourselves and others, our sense of compassion will become stronger and ultimately make our lives better. If we focus on judgment and anger, our sense of resentment will grow and ultimately make our lives far less pleasant.

As I mentioned, I took a Loving Kindness Meditation class when my mother was in the throes of Alzheimer's. Somehow, through the tools in this course, I was able to be compassionate with myself and genuinely happy in spite of my stress and sorrow. I found a calm centre in myself which kept me steady amidst the storms pounding through my life at that moment.

Along the way, I learned these other strategies to build inner strength:

    a. Breathe. It's amazing how easy it is to get tense; I think I spent about two years with tense shoulders. Just focusing on your breath and counting ten breaths can help you relax and be in the moment.

    b. Be present. It's easy to spend all your time wrapped up in the challenges you're experiencing. Sometimes it is necessary to pull your thoughts away from the challenges. Be fully present where you are - notice sights, sounds, tune in to conversations. Force yourself to notice what is good and sweet in the moment.

    c. Get out in nature. Go for a walk. Just 30 minutes a day in nature has positive effects on your mental and physical health. Getting out might feel like too much work, but I promise that if you do it, you will feel much better.

    d. Do something for yourself every day. After my brother died, I took two weeks off from work because I was so overwhelmed with grief. During that time, I made a rule that I had to leave the house every day and do some form of exercise. 15 minutes was all I asked of myself. The act of getting out and going for a walk or a swim was really good for me, and once I was out, I would often do more.

e. Nurture yourself. Go for walks, go see movies, take long hot baths, eat really good chocolate, or buy yourself flowers. This is what I did to nourish my soul during the difficult times. Think about what gives you comfort and take the time to do it. Plan something to look forward to.

f. Cut yourself some slack. You can't do everything you normally would be able to. You might have to start saying no. I have an overly developed sense of responsibility combined with a desire to go out and have many adventures. That means I say yes to almost everything! But when I was going through really challenging emotional experiences, it was exhausting. I had to start saying no. I didn't have the energy to give. I had to choose to do things that nurtured me. I learned that I could leave everything else, and it would still be there when I was ready.

g. Enjoy the good moments. Laugh. Sometimes there is guilt associated with a moment of joy in the midst of misery and pain. Laughter and pleasure are so important, even more important when we are swamped with sorrow. Allow yourself to enjoy those moments. They will nourish you and help you get through everything you have to face. Laughter is also incredibly good for our immune system. When my mother was battling cancer, she watched comedy shows every day and she's certain it helped her fight the cancer. No matter what you are going through, make time to laugh, to deeply feel and enjoy the pleasure in your life.

7. Reframe the situation

I was 33 and single when my mom died at age 59. So many people kept saying, "You're so young. She was so young!" Of course a part of me agreed and felt so sad that she would never get to meet my yet-to-be-found husband or my long-dreamt-of children. But I kept reframing it to remind myself that I had an extra 22 years with her because she should have died when I was 11.

We always have a choice about how we perceive a situation. We can focus on the negative aspects, or we can choose to focus on what good came of the situation, or what we learned from it. This doesn't diminish the sorrow but layers it with gratitude instead of self-pity.

The other thing to reframe is our relationship with the difficult stuff. Don't let it define you. You are more than your illness, your divorce, your loss, your upbringing, or your caregiving role. While it can be incredibly consuming - and it's tempting to overly identify with what you are going through - you are not your situation. You are yourself. When I was caring for my mom, it took up every spare moment I had, even intruding into the work sphere. I was hesitant to tell my manager about the situation for a few months since I was new to my job and didn't want him to see me as the woman with the mother with Alzheimer's. I eventually told him when my mom's needs started to interfere with the demands of my work, and thankfully, he was compassionate and understanding.

I still try to keep my challenges from interfering with my work life or identifying me. When I'm at work or with acquaintances, I prefer to focus on that which is going well in my life - my two young children, my writing, my consulting work. This shifts my focus to other parts of my life.

Our experiences do not define us unless we choose to let them. Loss can leave us empty or give us new meaning; betrayal can destroy our faith in humanity or push us to be strong enough to trust again. It's not the event - it's our response that defines us. We have to dig deep, stand in the eye of the storm, be in the centre of the pain, and then choose who we will become in the face of it. Then we have to put it behind us, so it does not become us. Instead, our experience becomes part of us, but it does not define who we are.

8. Practice gratitude

When really tough stuff happens in our lives, it can feel impossible to find anything to be grateful for. Yet there always is something to be thankful for, even in the darkest moments. Growing up with a brother who couldn't speak or eat or control his body made me realize how fortunate I was that my body functioned, and what a gift it was to do even the most basic things. Learning to appreciate what one is given helps you to remember the goodness amidst the darkness.

When my mom had Alzheimer's, I kept reminding myself, "Steph, this is the best it will be. Tomorrow or next week, she will be worse. Enjoy what you have now while still grieving for what you are losing". It was a complicated dance, but it helped me avoid getting swallowed up in the despair of losing her. Yes, I felt deep sorrow, but I also had gratitude for the small moments we had together.

While I was going through these experiences, I chose to keep a gratitude journal. Every night I wrote down three things I was grateful for. This practice helped me connect with what was feeding my spirit rather than what was draining it; it helped me remind myself of all the good things that were also occurring in my life. The night before I got the phone call that my brother had mere hours left to live I had written a particularly long list – 100 things I felt grateful for. I needed that list more than ever to bring to mind the good things in my life; it served as a tool to help me climb back up out of the well of grief I entered after losing him.

No matter what life delivers, there is always something to be grateful for. Very often difficult experiences can highlight what we have to be truly grateful for – good friends who come through for us, a hug from someone we love, a warm meal, a hot bath, sunshine, clean air.

9. Keep going

Life can be heart wrenching. It is really awful sometimes. And then, it gets better. You have to tough it out through those hard times and keep going until it gets better. I've been so inspired by watching my brother with bipolar disorder pull the pieces of his life back together time and time again when everything has fallen apart. He just doesn't quit. I look at him and think, "Yes, my life can be overwhelming, but his is even more challenging, and he pushes through." He inspires me to keep going. So many people have been through hell and they have come out on the other side. There was a dark moment in my life when my brother had just died, my boyfriend had dumped me, and I was heartbroken about my mother's Alzheimer's; I couldn't see that things could ever get better. But they did, slowly but surely, they did. Keep going. It will get better.

In Closing

One of the reasons I feel grateful for having had some difficult stuff in my life is that it helps me see what really matters and what my priorities are. What really matters is people and loving them well. That's the bottom line. Our time is short, and we don't know when it will end. I learned that early on. I feel grateful that I've been able to live a full and rich life with my priorities in the right place.

The morning I got the phone call that my brother was dying I was stressing out about a presentation I had to give. The day we got my mother's Alzheimer's diagnosis I was worried about a project at work. Those worries quickly disappeared in the face of something much bigger and more important. The key is to be able to hold on to this clarity when life gets better.

My perspective on life has changed because of my many experiences with my family. I try not to sweat the small stuff; I appreciate the times when life flows easily; every day I feel grateful that my kids are healthy; I take risks and try new things because I can. I'm alive, in a strong able body, and with a strong able mind. This is a gift. I have a responsibility to use it well, to live a good life, and to share what I've learned with others.

I wish for you the strength to know that you can and will survive whatever comes your way, and to know how deeply loved and treasured you are by so many. I wish for you the courage to walk through the fires of your rage, to surrender to the stream of your sorrow, to have the courage to feel the pain of loss. Most of all, I wish for you that you do not let the difficult stuff define you. Do not let this unmoor you. You are who you have always been; nothing has changed even though everything has changed. The core of you remains. You are not lost. You will land again in your own soft centre. Until then, I wish you the strength to let go, to fully experience the depth of feelings, and then let them move through you. I have been there and I send you my love, my strength, and my courage. You can and will come through the difficult stuff – keep going, keep feeling, keep reaching out for help and keep growing. One day you will notice as I did, that things have gotten easier. I hope these strategies help you thrive on the wild ride that is this beautiful life.

Acknowledgements:

My deepest gratitude to my editor Jacinda Fairholm who worked under ridiculous deadlines to help me get this book published. Thanks also to Ares Jun for designing the book, to Sonja Larsen for her valuable feedback, and to Railene Langdon (bluepixeldesign.com) for all of her technological support in getting my blog up and running and making sure this book can get to you in the digital world. My gratitude also goes to my husband Andrew Berryman for taking the children out in the pouring rain for hours on end so I could complete this book.

Printed in Great Britain
by Amazon

70023620R00021